A TRUE BOOK

W9-CNK-859

My United States
Delaware

MELISSA MCDANIEL

Children's Press®
An Imprint of Scholastic Inc.

Content Consultant

James Wolfinger, PhD, Associate Dean and Professor
College of Education, DePaul University, Chicago, Illinois

Library of Congress Cataloging-in-Publication Data
Names: McDaniel, Melissa, 1964– author.
Title: Delaware / by Melissa McDaniel.
Description: New York : Children's Press, [2019] | Series: A true book | Includes bibliographical references
    and index.
Identifiers: LCCN 2018000496 | ISBN 9780531235577 (library binding) | ISBN 9780531250761 (pbk.)
Subjects: LCSH: Delaware—Juvenile literature.
Classification: LCC F164.3 .M37 2019 | DDC 975.1—dc23
LC record available at https://lccn.loc.gov/2018000496

Photographs ©: cover: Jon Bilous/Alamy Images; back cover bottom: Kent Kobersteen/Getty Images; back cover ribbon: AliceLiddelle/Getty Images; 3 bottom: Maurice Savage/Alamy Images; 3 map: Jim McMahon/Mapman ®; 4 left: Leighton Photography & Imaging/Shutterstock; 4 right: myistock88/iStockphoto; 5 top: Kevin Fleming/Getty Images; 5 bottom: ANTONIO BALAGUER SOLER/123RF; 7 top: Mira/Alamy Images; 7 center top: Kevin Fleming/Getty Images; 7 center bottom: Kevin Fleming/Getty Images; 7 bottom: Dale Clifton/DiscoverSea Museum; 8-9: Michael Melford/Getty Images; 11: George Grall/Getty Images; 12: Photo by Scott Dunn/Getty Images; 13: Zachary Frank/Alamy Images; 14: David Osberg/iStockphoto; 15: Barrie Britton/Nature Picture Library; 16-17: Dennis Macdonald/Getty Images; 19: Noah Scialom/Epa/REX/Shutterstock; 20: Tigatelu/Dreamstime; 22 right: grebeshkovmaxim/Shutterstock; 22 left: grebeshkovmaxim/Shutterstock; 23 bottom left: ANTONIO BALAGUER SOLER/123RF; 23 top right: Joel Sartore/Getty Images; 23 bottom right: Lintao Zhang/Getty Images; 23 center left: Jim Zipp/Science Source; 23 top left: Leighton Photography & Imaging/Shutterstock; 23 center right: myistock88/iStockphoto; 24-25: VCG Wilson/Corbis/Getty Images; 27: Kevin Fleming/Getty Images; 29: Ben Gabbe/Stringer/Getty Images; 30 bottom: Kevin Fleming/Getty Images; 30 top: Ben Gabbe/Stringer/Getty Images; 31 left: SOMATUSCAN/iStockphoto; 31 right: Robert Goebel/Alamy Images; 32: Lewis Hine/The Granger Collection; 33: Courtesy of the Delaware Historical Society; 34-35: Randy Duchaine/Alamy Images; 36: Chris Trotman/Getty Images; 37: Democrat and Chronicle/USA TODAY Network; 38: Jake Rajs/Getty Images; 39: Kevin Fleming/Getty Images; 40 inset: Zolotaosen/iStockphoto; 40 background: PepitoPhotos/iStockphoto; 41: Kent County Tourism Corporation; 42 top left: Sarin Images/The Granger Collection; 42 top right: AP Images; 42 bottom center: Stewart Cook/REX/Shutterstock; 42 bottom right: Michael Cuscuna/Mosaic Images/Corbis/Getty Images; 42 bottom left: Ron Galella, Ltd./WireImage/Getty Images; 43 top: David Lienemann/The White House/Getty Images; 43 center right: Patrick McMullan/Getty Images; 43 center left: Laura Novak; 43 bottom left: Earl Gibson III/Getty Images; 43 bottom right: Jonathan Newton/The Washington Post/Getty Images; 44 bottom left: Popartic/iStockphoto; 44 top: Delaware State Fair; 44 bottom right: Frederik Christoffersen/iStockphoto; 45 top: Kate Timbers/Shutterstock; 45 bottom: SOMATUSCAN/iStockphoto.

Maps by Map Hero, Inc.

No part of this publication may be reproduced in whole or in part, or stored in a retrieval system, or transmitted in any form or by any means, electronic, mechanical, photocopying, recording, or otherwise, without written permission of the publisher. For information regarding permission, write to Scholastic Inc., Attention: Permissions Department, 557 Broadway, New York, NY 10012.
© 2019 Scholastic Inc.

All rights reserved. Published in 2019 by Children's Press, an imprint of Scholastic Inc.
Printed in North Mankato, MN, USA 113

SCHOLASTIC, CHILDREN'S PRESS, A TRUE BOOK™, and associated logos are trademarks and/or registered trademarks of Scholastic Inc.

Scholastic Inc., 557 Broadway, New York, NY 10012

1 2 3 4 5 6 7 8 9 10 R 28 27 26 25 24 23 22 21 20 19

Front cover: Lightship Overfalls

Back cover: Steam engine on Wilmington and Western Railroad

Welcome to Delaware

Find the Truth!

Everything you are about to read is true *except* for one of the sentences on this page.

Which one is **TRUE**?

T or F Delaware was the first state to outlaw slavery.

T or F Delaware was the first state to approve the U.S. Constitution.

Find the answers in this book.

Key Facts

Capital: Dover

Estimated population as of 2017: 961,939

Nicknames: First State, Diamond State

Biggest cities: Wilmington, Dover, Newark

UNITED STATES

Delaware

Contents

THE BIG TRUTH!

Peach
blossom

What Represents Delaware?

Tiger swallowtail
butterfly

4

Rehoboth Beach

3 History

How did Delaware become
the state it is today?

4 Culture

What do the people of Delaware
do for work and fun?

Blue Hen Chicken

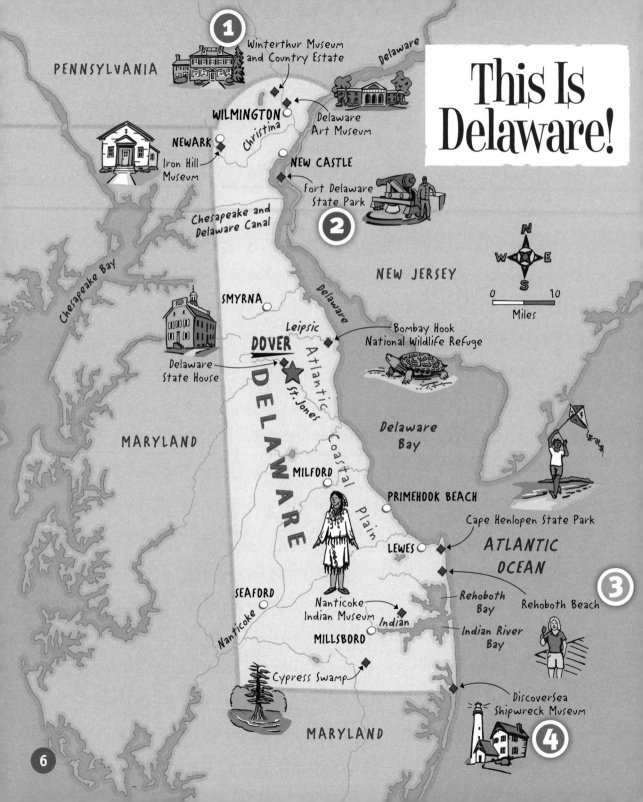

This Is Delaware!

PENNSYLVANIA

1 Winterthur Museum and Country Estate

Delaware

WILMINGTON

Delaware Art Museum

NEWARK

Iron Hill Museum

Christina

NEW CASTLE

2 Fort Delaware State Park

Chesapeake and Delaware Canal

Chesapeake Bay

MARYLAND

SMYRNA

Delaware

Leipsic

Bombay Hook National Wildlife Refuge

DOVER

St. Jones

Delaware State House

DELAWARE

Atlantic

Coastal Plain

NEW JERSEY

N W E S

0   10
Miles

Delaware Bay

MILFORD

PRIMEHOOK BEACH

Cape Henlopen State Park

LEWES

ATLANTIC OCEAN

3

Nanticoke Indian Museum

Indian

SEAFORD

Nanticoke

MILLSBORO

Rehoboth Bay

Rehoboth Beach

Indian River Bay

Cypress Swamp

DiscoverSea Shipwreck Museum

4

MARYLAND

1 Winterthur Museum

This estate in northern Delaware was once the grand home of Henry Francis du Pont. Du Pont was a collector of art and furniture. Today, the home is a museum featuring 175 carefully decorated rooms reflecting different time periods and styles.

2 Fort Delaware State Park

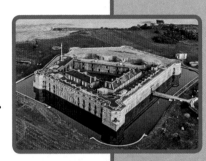

Fort Delaware sits on Pea Patch Island in the Delaware River. This fortress held **Confederate** prisoners during the Civil War. Today, costumed guides explain what life was like in the fort in 1864.

3 Rehoboth Beach

This beach is famed for its clean water, beautiful sand, and fun boardwalk. Visitors can build sandcastles or take a boat ride to see dolphins leaping above the ocean waves.

4 DiscoverSea Shipwreck Museum

This museum in the southeastern corner of the state displays items brought up from shipwrecks found at the bottom of the sea. Its exhibits include jewelry, bowls, and more.

Located on the border between Delaware and Pennsylvania, the Brandywine Valley is famous for its many gardens, museums, and historic mansions.

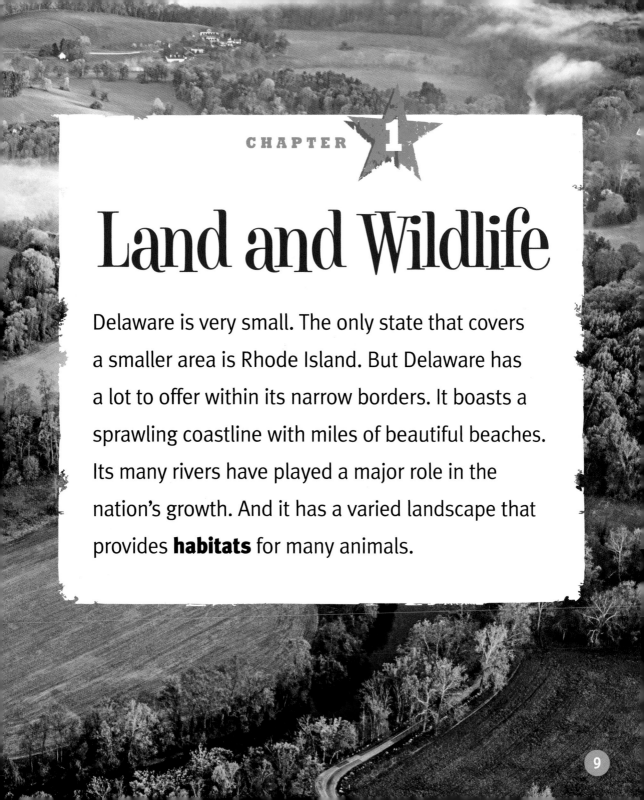

CHAPTER 1

Land and Wildlife

Delaware is very small. The only state that covers a smaller area is Rhode Island. But Delaware has a lot to offer within its narrow borders. It boasts a sprawling coastline with miles of beautiful beaches. Its many rivers have played a major role in the nation's growth. And it has a varied landscape that provides **habitats** for many animals.

The Lay of the Land

Delaware hugs the sea. Its eastern edge lies along the Delaware Bay and the Atlantic Ocean. Maryland borders the state on the west and south, while Pennsylvania forms the state's tiny northern border. New Jersey is positioned across the Delaware Bay to the east.

Much of the shoreline of the Delaware Bay is marshy. Farther south along the open ocean are broad beaches. Most of the land in Delaware is flat plains. Only in the north are there rolling hills.

This map shows where the higher (orange) and lower (green) areas are in Delaware.

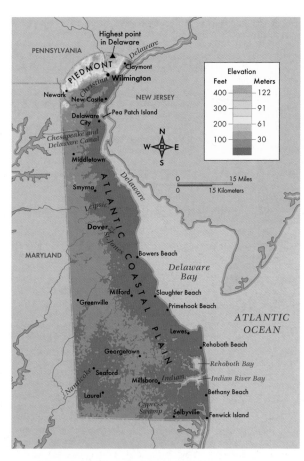

A flock of dunlins passes over the water at Bombay Hook National Wildlife Refuge.

Bombay Hook National Wildlife Refuge

Bombay Hook is a large stretch of **salt marsh** along the Delaware Bay. No matter the time of year, it is one of the best places in Delaware to spot birds. Bombay Hook is an important stopping point for many birds on their long **migration** along the East Coast. More than 300 bird species feed on the plentiful fish, crab, and other creatures found there. In the fall, 150,000 ducks and snow geese fill the sky. In spring, shorebirds such as plovers spread across the area's **mudflats**.

11

MAXIMUM TEMPERATURE
110°F

MINIMUM TEMPERATURE
-17°F

Rehoboth Beach is one of Delaware's most popular beaches. It draws huge crowds on hot summer days.

Warm and Wet

Delaware summers are warm and humid. July is the hottest month, with temperatures often reaching about 85 degrees Fahrenheit (29 degrees Celsius). When it's that hot, many Delawareans head to the beach to cool off in the water. The breezes off the ocean also help make the heat more tolerable. Rain is common throughout the year. It falls about one out of every three days. Winters are fairly mild, with only a few snowy days per year.

Plants

Different kinds of trees and plants grow in different parts of Delaware. In the north, the forests are filled with hardwood trees such as oaks and maples. Evergreen trees such as cedars and pines grow along the coast. In the swamps of the south are majestic bald cypress trees. These huge trees can grow up out of the water. Reeds, lilies, orchids, and hibiscus plants flourish along Delaware's many ponds and marshes.

Kayaking is a popular activity at Trap Pond State Park.

Animals

Red foxes sometimes leave their forest homes and venture into Delaware's towns, where they eat garbage and pet food.

Many creatures live in the forests and fields of Delaware. In the forests, deer munch on leaves, while chipmunks skitter from the ground to the treetops. In the fields, foxes prey on rabbits, mice, and other small animals that live there. Hundreds of species of birds make Delaware their home. Cardinals and warblers flit through the forest. In the marshes, herons, egrets, and terns hunt for insects, fish, and other food.

From Sea to Shore

Shellfish such as oysters, clams, and crabs thrive in Delaware Bay. The bay is home to the world's largest population of horseshoe crabs. In spring, millions of these crabs come ashore to lay eggs. The eggs serve as vital food for migrating birds. The red knot is a bird the size of a robin. It migrates all the way from South America to the Arctic. Without gorging on horseshoe crab eggs, red knots would not be able to complete their journey.

Each spring, Mispillion Harbor hosts a festival celebrating the annual gathering of horseshoe crabs.

Because Delaware was the first state, Dover was the first state capital in the nation.

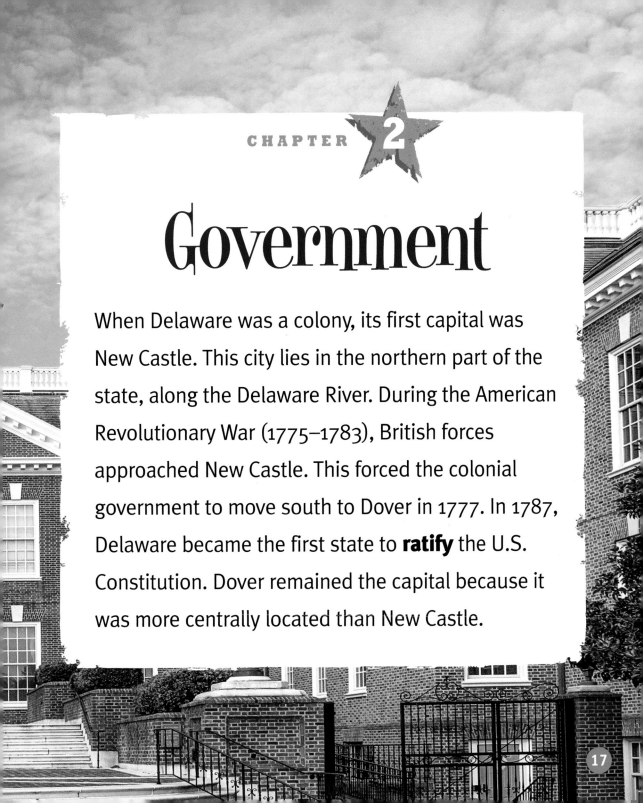

CHAPTER 2

Government

When Delaware was a colony, its first capital was New Castle. This city lies in the northern part of the state, along the Delaware River. During the American Revolutionary War (1775–1783), British forces approached New Castle. This forced the colonial government to move south to Dover in 1777. In 1787, Delaware became the first state to **ratify** the U.S. Constitution. Dover remained the capital because it was more centrally located than New Castle.

State Government Basics

Delaware's government is divided into three branches. The executive branch runs the government and carries out the state laws. The legislative branch makes laws for the state. It consists of a Senate and a House of Representatives. The state courts make up the judicial branch. The courts settle disputes and try people charged with crimes.

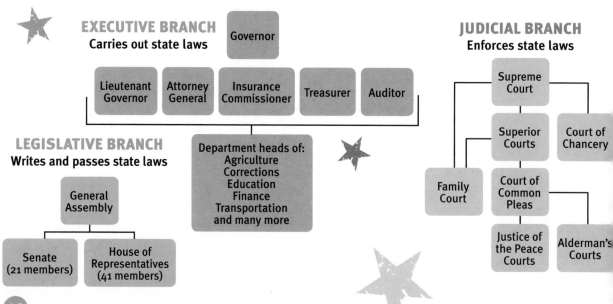

DELAWARE'S STATE GOVERNMENT

EXECUTIVE BRANCH
Carries out state laws

Governor

Lieutenant Governor | Attorney General | Insurance Commissioner | Treasurer | Auditor

LEGISLATIVE BRANCH
Writes and passes state laws

Department heads of:
Agriculture
Corrections
Education
Finance
Transportation
and many more

General Assembly

Senate (21 members) | House of Representatives (41 members)

JUDICIAL BRANCH
Enforces state laws

Supreme Court

Superior Courts | Court of Chancery

Family Court | Court of Common Pleas

Justice of the Peace Courts | Alderman's Courts

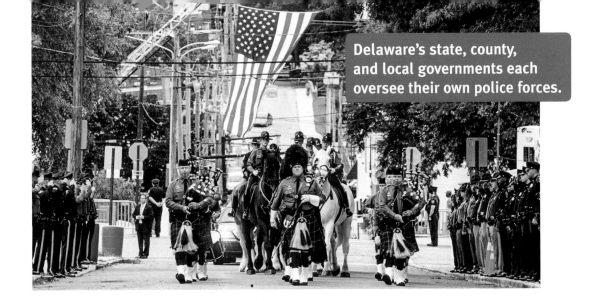

Delaware's state, county, and local governments each oversee their own police forces.

Three Counties

All states are divided into smaller units that are usually called counties. Delaware has just three counties: New Castle, Kent, and Sussex. No other state has such a small number of counties. In many states, counties have their own court systems and law enforcement. Delaware is so small, however, that the state government handles most of this. Delaware county governments run the local sewer systems. They also ensure that buildings are constructed safely and decide where they can be built.

Delaware in the National Government

Each state elects officials to represent it in the U.S. Congress. Like every state, Delaware has two senators. The U.S. House of Representatives relies on a state's population to determine its numbers. Delaware has one representative in the House.

Every four years, states vote on the next U.S. president. Each state is granted a number of electoral votes based on its number of members in Congress. With two senators and one representative, Delaware has three electoral votes.

With three electoral votes, Delaware's voice in presidential elections is below average compared to other states.

The People of Delaware

Elected officials in Delaware represent a population with a range of interests, lifestyles, and backgrounds.

Ethnicity (2016 estimates)

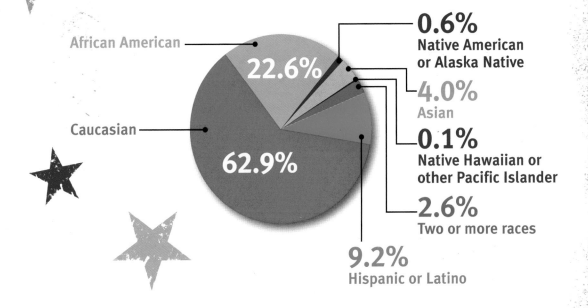

African American — 22.6%

Caucasian — 62.9%

0.6%
Native American or Alaska Native

4.0%
Asian

0.1%
Native Hawaiian or other Pacific Islander

2.6%
Two or more races

9.2%
Hispanic or Latino

9% were born in another country.

71% own their own homes.

31% have a bachelor's degree or higher.

13% speak a language other than English at home.

89% graduated from high school.

18% are over age 65.

What Represents Delaware?

States choose specific animals, plants, and objects to represent the values and characteristics of the land and its people. Find out why these symbols were chosen to represent Delaware or discover surprising curiosities about them.

Seal

Delaware's state seal depicts a farmer and a soldier. It also shows other symbols of the state's agricultural history, including an ox, wheat, and corn. The blue stripe represents the Delaware River, and the three years are important dates in Delaware's history. Delaware formed its first government in 1704. The American colonies declared independence in 1776. And Delaware became the first state in 1787.

Flag

Delaware's state flag shows a diamond in a pale yellow color called buff. The diamond is set against a blue field. Blue and buff were the colors of George Washington's uniform during the American Revolution. Inside the diamond are the images from the state seal.

Tiger Swallowtail

STATE BUTTERFLY

This beautiful butterfly is named for the black stripes on its bright-yellow body. It is common all along the East Coast.

Horseshoe Crab

STATE MARINE ANIMAL

Delaware Bay is home to more horseshoe crabs than anywhere else in the world.

American Holly

STATE TREE

The American holly has dark, thorny leaves and bright-red berries. It grows well in Delaware's moist lowlands and sandy soil.

Peach Blossom

STATE FLOWER

The peach blossom was named the state flower in 1895. At the time, Delaware was the leading peach-producing state in the nation.

Blue Hen Chicken

STATE BIRD

The blue hen is a type of chicken that often has blue feathers and is known for its strength and fierceness. During the American Revolution, an officer from Delaware bred blue hens, and they became a symbol for the state's troops.

Weakfish

STATE FISH

Weakfish live in the waters off of Delaware. They are a popular catch for local fishers.

During the Revolutionary War, the uniform of Delaware's soldiers was eventually chosen as the uniform for the entire American army.

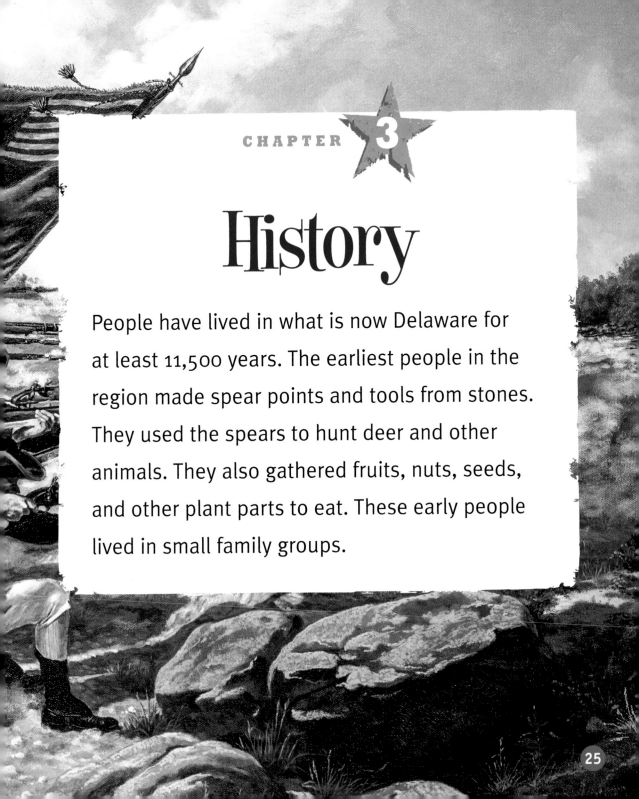

CHAPTER 3

History

People have lived in what is now Delaware for at least 11,500 years. The earliest people in the region made spear points and tools from stones. They used the spears to hunt deer and other animals. They also gathered fruits, nuts, seeds, and other plant parts to eat. These early people lived in small family groups.

The Woodland Culture

By about 3000 BCE, the Woodland culture had developed in the region. Woodland people made clay pottery. They lived near rivers and marshes in houses called wigwams. These homes were made of branches and bark. Oysters and other shellfish were important sources of food. The Woodland people gathered them along Delaware's coast. By the 1400s CE, other Native American cultures had arisen in what is now Delaware.

This map shows some of the major tribes that lived in what is now Delaware before Europeans came.

A Nanticoke man performs a traditional dance.

Native American Life

The two main Native American cultures in Delaware were the Lenape and the Nanticoke. The Lenape lived in the north, and the Nanticoke lived in the south. Both groups hunted, fished, and gathered plants. They also eventually farmed beans, squash, corn, and sunflowers. The Lenape and Nanticoke also both spoke versions of the Algonquian language.

Settlement and Statehood

In 1609, Englishman Henry Hudson and his crew steered their ship into the Delaware Bay. They were the first Europeans to reach the area. Delaware's first European settlement was not established until 1631, when Holland started Zwaanendael, in the south. In the following decades, Holland, Sweden, and England fought over the region. Finally, England gained control.

In 1610, Englishman Samuel Argall named the region Delaware, after Lord De La Warr, the governor of the Virginia colony.

Fort Göteborg
Philadelphia
Delaware
Fort Christina
Christina
Fort Casimir
(Fort Trinity)
Fort Nya Elfsborg
Leipsic
Delaware
St. Jones
Delaware Bay
Nanticoke
Indian
ATLANTIC OCEAN

← Henry Hudson, 1609
← Samuel Argall, 1610
▥ Fort
● Present-day city
▨ Present-day state of Delaware

N
W-E
S

0   15 Miles
0   15 Kilometers

This map shows the routes taken by the first European explorers to reach present-day Delaware.

Henry Hudson meets with Native Americans after landing in the Delaware Bay.

Delaware became one of 13 English colonies lined up along the East Coast. By the 1770s, many colonists were unhappy with the English government. The American Revolution began in 1775. The following year, Delawarean Caesar Rodney made a heroic ride to Philadelphia, Pennsylvania, to decide whether Delaware would vote for independence. Even though he was seriously ill, he made it to the meeting. Without Rodney, the Declaration of Independence might not have passed. In 1787, Delaware became the first state.

Industry Grows

By the end of the 1700s, farming was the main business in Delaware. But industry soon began to grow. Delawareans built cloth, paper, and flour mills on the state's swift rivers. There were soon 130 flour mills near Wilmington. The Chesapeake and Delaware Canal opened in 1829, providing ships a much faster route from Wilmington to Baltimore, Maryland, and other big cities.

Timeline of Delaware Events

1400s CE
Lenape and Nanticoke peoples live in what is now Delaware.

1631
The Dutch establish the first European settlement in Delaware.

9500 BCE → 1400s CE → 1609 → 1631

9500 BCE
The first people arrive in Delaware.

1609
Henry Hudson leads the first Europeans into Delaware Bay.

Slavery and Freedom

By the early 1800s, slavery was ending in the Northern states but remained legal in Delaware and the Southern states. Many Delawareans helped enslaved people escape to the North on the **Underground Railroad**. But Delaware remained a slave state until the end of the Civil War (1861–1865), when slavery was outlawed throughout the nation.

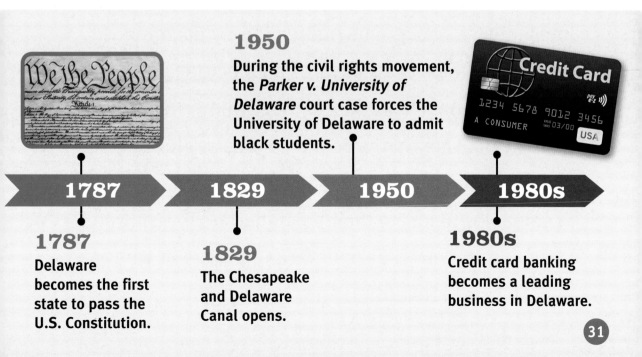

1950

During the civil rights movement, the *Parker v. University of Delaware* court case forces the University of Delaware to admit black students.

1787 > **1829** > **1950** > **1980s**

1787

Delaware becomes the first state to pass the U.S. Constitution.

1829

The Chesapeake and Delaware Canal opens.

1980s

Credit card banking becomes a leading business in Delaware.

Newsboys were young workers hired to sell newspapers in Wilmington and other cities in the early 20th century.

The 20th Century

Early in the 20th century, Delaware's economy thrived on industry. Immigrants poured into Wilmington to work in the city's shipyards and factories. The DuPont Company produced gunpowder, chemicals, and nylon. Later in the century, industry slowed. The state tried to revive its economy by encouraging companies to locate their headquarters in Delaware. As a result, many banks now run their credit card operations in Delaware.

Breaking Barriers

In the early 20th century, African Americans were legally barred from many schools and businesses. They had to fight to gain equal rights. In Delaware, Louis Redding was at the forefront of this fight. Redding had grown up going to **segregated** schools in Wilmington. He attended Harvard Law School and in 1929 became the first African American lawyer in Delaware. He often worked on cases that challenged segregation. In 1950, Redding won the *Parker v. University of Delaware* case, forcing the University of Delaware to admit black students.

The Delaware Art Museum in Wilmington has a collection of more than 12,000 pieces of artwork.

Catherine A. Fusco Grand

RE ART MUSE

CHAPTER 4

Culture

Delaware has inspired many artists and writers. Artist N. C. Wyeth, his son Andrew, and his grandson Jamie all painted the people and sights of northern Delaware, among other subjects. Christopher Castellani draws on his family's Italian immigrant experience in Wilmington to write novels such as *The Saint of Lost Things*. Delaware author Lara M. Zeises writes novels for teens, including *Contents Under Pressure* and *Bringing Up the Bones*.

Dover International Speedway has hosted races since 1969.

Sports Fans

Delaware is a small state with small cities, so it has no major league sports teams. Delawareans instead cheer for the University of Delaware Fightin' Blue Hens football team. Even more popular is NASCAR racing. Nearly 100,000 people fill the stands at Dover International Speedway on race days. Lots of people also head to Dover Downs racetrack to watch horse racing.

Delaware Celebrations

Delaware festivals often draw people to the state's beaches. At the Rehoboth Beach Sandcastle Contest, teams compete to sculpt spectacular mermaids, dolphins, and more. In April, colorful kites fill the air at the Great Delaware Kite Festival. Other festivals honor the heritage of Delawareans. The August Quarterly Festival in Wilmington celebrates African American history and life.

The Great Delaware Kite Festival celebrated its 50th anniversary in 2018.

Delaware farmers produce about 215 million meat chickens, or broilers, each year.

Off to Work

A lot of the land in Delaware is devoted to agriculture. Chickens are the state's most valuable agricultural product. Delaware farmers also grow soybeans and corn. Other Delawareans head to the water for work. They catch lobsters and crabs and collect oysters and clams. Many people in Delaware work at companies that produce chemicals or medicines. Lots of other Delawareans work in banks, schools, and other important service industries.

Tourists and locals gather on a Delaware beach to watch a Fourth of July fireworks display.

Changing Jobs

Tourism is a growing part of Delaware's economy. People are flocking to southern Delaware's beautiful beaches. This creates lots of jobs for people working in hotels, restaurants, and shops. Increasingly, older people are choosing to retire in Delaware. This means there are more jobs in health care. It also means the coastal region needs more businesses like banks and grocery stores to serve year-round residents.

Let's Eat

Delawareans eat many locally grown foods. Seafood is popular, especially crab. Peaches, the state fruit, are used in pie and cake. They are also delicious on their own! Local apples are used in apple butter and apple cider doughnuts. At the boardwalk, beachgoers enjoy French fries topped with vinegar. Those who prefer something sweet chew on sticky saltwater taffy.

 ## Crab Cakes

Ask an adult to help you!

These crispy, fried cakes are a Delaware delicacy!

Ingredients

1 egg
3 tablespoons mayonnaise
4 teaspoons lemon juice
1 tablespoon minced green onions

1 dash hot sauce
8 ounces crabmeat
$1/2$ cup crushed crackers
1 tablespoon butter

Directions

Whisk together the egg, mayonnaise, lemon juice, onions, and hot sauce in a bowl. Gently stir in the crabmeat and crackers. Form the mixture into 4 patties. Heat the butter in a skillet over medium heat. Cook the patties until golden brown, about 5 minutes on each side. Enjoy!

Killens Pond State Park is a popular spot to go fishing.

Out and About

Whether you're visiting on vacation or a longtime resident, there's a lot to do in Delaware. You can explore old cities and marvel at grand mansions. You can hike around ponds or play some arcade games. You can fish in the ocean or watch horseshoe crabs crawl from beneath the waves onto the beach. And you can lie in the sand or play in the waves—the perfect end to a perfect day. ★

Famous People

Annie Jump Cannon

(1863–1941) was an astronomer who worked at Harvard College Observatory in Massachusetts. During her career, she categorized thousands of stars. Her system for classifying stars is still used today. She was from Dover.

Wallace Carothers

(1896–1937) was a brilliant chemist and inventor who worked for the DuPont Company. He led the group that invented nylon and neoprene.

Cab Calloway

(1907–1994) was a jazz singer and songwriter who also appeared in many films and stage musicals. He lived in Delaware in his later years, and there is a performing arts high school named after him in Delaware.

Henry Heimlich

(1920–2016) was a surgeon who invented a method for saving people who are choking. This procedure is now known as the Heimlich maneuver. He was born in Wilmington.

Clifford Brown

(1930–1956) was a jazz trumpeter famed for his quick and graceful style. He was from Wilmington.

Joseph Biden Jr.

(1942–) was a U.S. senator from Delaware for 36 years before serving as vice president under President Barack Obama from 2009 to 2017.

Susan Stroman

(1954–) is a theater director and choreographer. She has won five Tony Awards for her work on shows such as *The Producers* and *Crazy for You*.

Lara M. Zeises

(1976–) is a novelist who writes books for young adults. Her works include *Bringing Up the Bones* and *Contents Under Pressure*. She set many of her novels in Delaware, where she has lived since she was a child.

Aubrey Plaza

(1984–) is an actor and comedian best known for her work on the TV shows *Parks and Recreation* and *Legion*. She is from Wilmington.

Elena Delle Donne

(1989–) is a pro basketball star in the Women's National Basketball Association (WNBA). She won the league's Rookie of the Year award in 2013 and was named its Most Valuable Player in 2015. She is from Wilmington.

Did You Know That...

About 300,000 people attend the Delaware State Fair every year. That's almost one out of every three people in the state.

Delaware is a tiny state. At its widest, it is only 35 miles (56 kilometers) from east to west. At its narrowest, it is just 9 miles (14 km) across.

There are no diamond mines in Delaware, yet one of the state's nicknames is the Diamond State. Legend traces this nickname to President Thomas Jefferson. It is said that he described Delaware as a jewel among the states because of its important location along the coast.

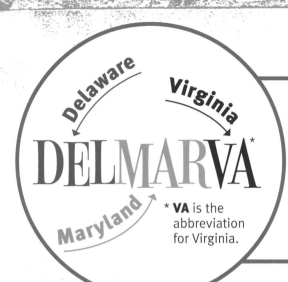

Delaware
Virginia
DELMARVA*
Maryland

* **VA** is the abbreviation for Virginia.

Delaware is located on the Delmarva **Peninsula**, which also includes parts of Maryland and Virginia. The peninsula's name comes from combining the names of all three states.

Delaware's northern border with Pennsylvania is called the 12-mile circle. It is an arc, or a section of a circle. The center of the circle is the courthouse (shown here) in New Castle.

Did you find the truth?

F Delaware was the first state to outlaw slavery.

T Delaware was the first state to approve the U.S. Constitution.

Resources

Books

Cunningham, Kevin. *The Delaware Colony.* New York: Children's Press, 2012.

Heinrichs, Ann. *Delaware.* New York: Children's Press, 2015.

Rozett, Louise (ed.). *Fast Facts About the 50 States: Plus Puerto Rico and Washington, D.C.* New York: Children's Press, 2010.

Schnell, Lisa Kahn. *High Tide for Horseshoe Crabs.* Watertown, MA: Charlesbridge, 2015.

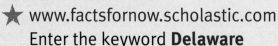

Visit this Scholastic website for more information on Delaware:
★ www.factsfornow.scholastic.com
Enter the keyword **Delaware**

Important Words

Confederate (kuhn-FED-ur-it) of or relating to the 11 Southern states that declared independence from the rest of the United States just before the Civil War

habitats (HAB-ih-tats) places where an animal or a plant is usually found

migration (mye-GRAY-shuhn) movement of people or animals from one region or habitat to another

mudflats (MUHD-flats) areas of land where large amounts of mud are left by rivers or other moving waters

peninsula (puh-NIN-suh-luh) a piece of land that sticks out from a larger landmass and is almost completely surrounded by water

ratify (RAT-uh-fye) to agree to or approve officially

salt marsh (SAWLT MARSH) flat land that is sometimes covered by salt water

segregated (SEG-rih-gay-tid) kept separate or apart

Underground Railroad (UN-dur-grownd RAYL-rohd) a network of people who secretly helped slaves from the South escape to free states in the North or to Canada before the Civil War

Index

Page numbers in **bold** indicate illustrations.

About the Author

Melissa McDaniel is the author of more than thirty books for young people. She was born in Portland, Oregon, and attended both Portland State University and the University of Washington. She now lives in New York City, where she works as a writer and editor.